# Souvenirs FROM THE ROADSIDE WEST

a personal collection by Richard Ansaldi

H

Harmony Books/New York

I dedicate this to John Anthes for his continued encouragement
and support.

I also extend my sincere appreciation to Cab Childress.

Inquiries should be addressed to:
Harmony Books, a division of Crown Publishers, Inc.
One Park Avenue, New York, New York 10016

Published simultaneously in Canada by General Publishing Co., Ltd.
Printed in Japan by Dai Nippon Printing Co., Ltd., Tokyo.

Grateful acknowledgement to Warner Bros. Music for permission to
reprint lyrics from "Short Grass" by Ian Tyson and Sylvia Fricker.
Copyright © 1966 Warner Bros. Inc. All Rights Reserved. Used by
permission.

Library of Congress Cataloging in Publication Data

Ansaldi, Richard.
    Souvenirs from the Roadside West.

    1. The West—Description and travel—1951-
2. Ansaldi, Richard.   I. Title.
F595.2.A56     917.8'04'3     77-27614
ISBN 0-517-53338-3
ISBN 0-517-53339-1 pbk.

# Contents

# 1 Prologue

The sun burns the snow, high on the mountains
It runs and it grows, as it falls
Silt and soil, down it boils
Down to the valleys, the gold river rolls
To the plains.

The rangeland lies high, up from the river
The coulees are dry, where the short grass grows
Fields of hay, cottonwood shade
Green patch of home, through the high dusty land
The river flows.

Early evening light, horseback is roping
The day fades away, the night rolls on
Lives of pride, men who ride
They keep the old skills, that came up the trail
From Mexico.

The long river winds, through green years and dry years
Brand 'em in the spring, ship 'em in the fall
A new colt foaled, the mare grows old
Cycle of changes, in this changeless land
Where the short grass grows.

—Ian Tyson and Sylvia Fricker

# 2 A western overture

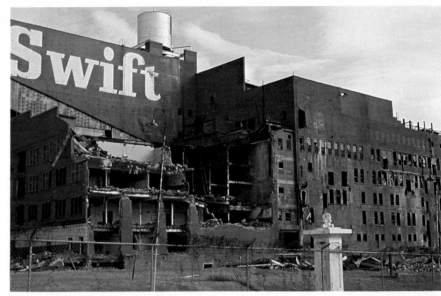

# 3
Symbols
and
sign
language

"In Santa Rosa, another old saying: For good food... the Club Cafe!

"That's a tough act to follow but the Club Cafe is for real. For over thirty years in the same location. Always the same good food, always the same friendly service.

"But we've been bypassed. A huge freeway zooms right past us. Radio's the only way we can tell you about ou sourdough biscuits. For those that have eaten them before, sourdough biscuits are a delight to rediscover. For those that have never eaten sourdough biscuits, you're in for a real treat. Fresh, hot, sourdough biscuits with honey is a tru experience. It's the goldrush days again. It's the daring mountain man. It's you at the Club Cafe munching sourdough biscuits."

"Of course, the Club offers more. We cut our own fresh meat. Our Mexican food is served with bronc-bustin', bear-clawin', fire-eatin' chili. We have five daily specials. We offer beef, beans, and biscuits. Try the Club Cafe for a happy treat...Highway 66 in the center of Santa Rosa."
—Radio ad from KSYZ, 1420 AM, Santa Rosa, New Mexico

"Picking a restaurant when you're traveling can be a real problem...with some that's real good food, and some that's not so good. Some is too expensive, some's too cheap. And then there's the Club Cafe...way out front with food, yet reasonably priced.

"Honest-to-goodness, authentic, sourdough biscuits ...hamburgers made with 100% ground beef...chicken-fried steaks made with tender, fresh meat and served with old-fashion, iron skillet gravy...homemade chili over great Mexican food...five daily luncheon specials from a dollar ninety-five. The Club Cafe IS different. The owner's a skilled butcher who knows how meat should be cut and prepared."

"And here's something else. The Club Cafe has the areas largest selection of gifts and souvenirs...all types and all price ranges...even the best cherry cider in the west. Feel welcome to come in and browse. There's plenty of parking at the Club Cafe...Highway 66, right in the center of town. Take any exit. You can't miss the Club Cafe ...Highway 66, downtown. And by the way, don't let that location scare you. There's no stop signs, no stop lights, no traffic congestion...just the best food in the area. Look for the Club!"

—Radio ad from KSYX, 1420 AM, Santa Rosa, New Mexico

# 4
## Searching for home-made pie

ANGEL'S VIEW

CAFE

The Angel's View Cafe is the last spot to eat in Albuquerque if you're driving west through town on old
Route 66. It's a small truck stop, high on the west mesa
overlooking the city. I had been eating there for some time
before I discovered their homemade cinnamon rolls. They
are loaded with raisins and cinnamon, and served hot with
butter. They are incredibly good and this fact is well known
by the regulars.

Josie, the daytime cook, arrives at dawn and spends
almost three hours making them from scratch. I had the
following conversation with her one morning as she prepared them.

*Where did you learn how to make cinnamon rolls?*

Well, I've cooked all my life.

*Is this a family recipe?*

No...no. My mother never did bake. You know, I think I
must have lived before. I'm not sure about reincarnation but
I think I must have. And other people who do exceptionally
well...I think they've lived before. I'm not sure about it...
reincarnation. I haven't decided whether it's a fact or just
fiction...but I notice people who are very musical or artis-
tic. When the soul leaves the body, that intelligence...it
seems to me, that intelligence gets incorporated in some
way...it seems to me.

*That's a nice way of looking at it.*

Yeah...because intelligence doesn't disintegrate.

*Do you start these at six every morning? Doesn't your shift begin at seven?*

I do this free...because we get too busy by the time those rolls rise. They've got to be taken care of...or I won't get 'em done. I've got to punch 'em down. I can punch 'em down anytime, in no time, and let 'em rise again.

*So this is all on your own time. Does the boss know what a good thing he's got going?*

[Laughing] I was sitting down one time having a coffee break when he says, "Holdin' that booth down are you?" I says, "You forget that I give you an hour free every mornin' ...five and six days a week." Then he just turns on his heels and leaves. [She laughs again]

*How long have you worked here?*

Let's see...for this owner I worked in here nine years...
and I worked a year and a half for another. I've only had
two jobs...two jobs! We had four restaurants and one
doughnut shop in Chicago at the same time.

*What happened to the restaurants in Chicago?*

We sold them and came to Albuquerque.

*You just decided to move?*

Well, we never had been this far west. And we came
through Albuquerque at night. And we never saw so many
neon lights and night life in ANY town, ANY where, of ANY
size.

*That was when?*

That was in '45. And my husband said, "Doesn't this look
like a livewire here!" I said, "I never saw as many lights."
And so we went on to San Diego. And we couldn't get
Albuquerque out of our minds. Well in fact, the year before that, he came here to take his vacation...in February.
And he called me and said, "Guess what?" He said, "I'm
playin' golf in short sleeves." FEBRUARY! And we were
snowed under in Chicago. Maybe what impressed us
though...we came in on "66" and probably this looked
like an oasis for us. Tucumcari wasn't anything. Nothing to
look at after we left the Oklahoma border. There wasn't
much. In those days this town was smothered with lights.

*Ever miss Chicago?*

Never did. Only thing I missed was the stores. Because
there you can get what you like at Christmas. I wanted to
buy my sister-in-law something nice. I went to the depart-
ment stores downtown. I wanted to buy her a peach colored
slip. You can buy anything in Chicago. And I went to the
two stores here and they didn't have anything but black
and white. Never will forget it. I could have stayed home.
That's all...black and white.

*You look like you really enjoy your work.*

I like to cook.

*That's good. Too many people are stuck with jobs they hate.*

Well if a person hates their job, they'll have all kinds of
ailments. Your body reflects your mind. I've seen waitresses
who hated to be a waitress...hated to wait on tables...
they break out.

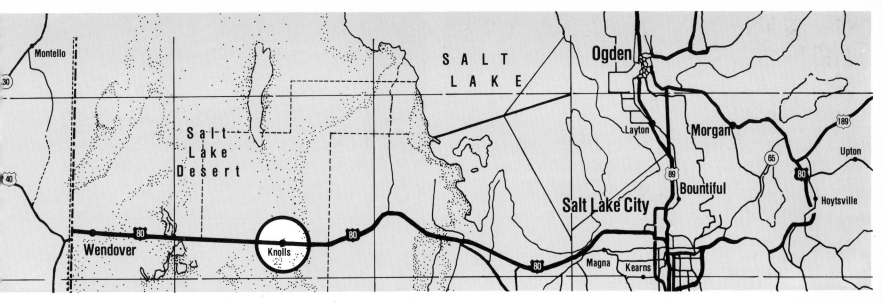

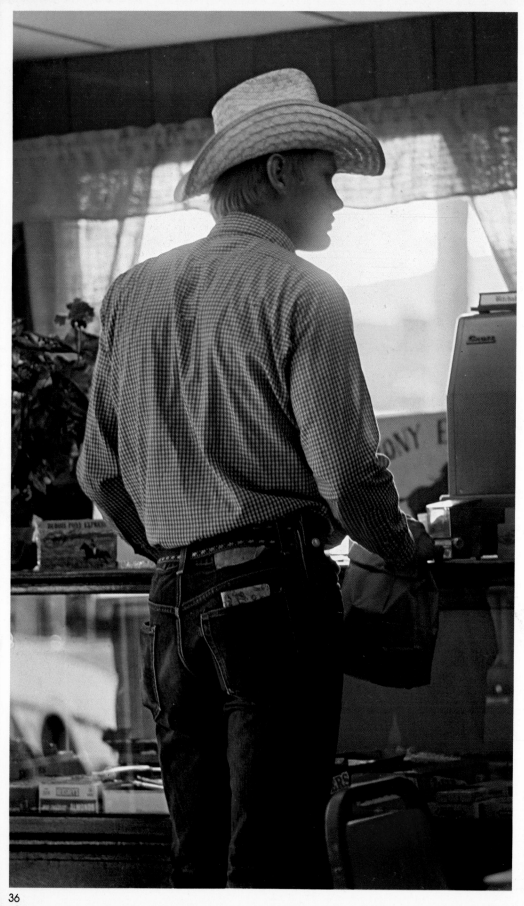

**E**unice Matthews has been selling cherry cider from a road-side stand in Alamogordo for the last seventeen years. I talked with her briefly two years ago and recently I returned to photograph her. The cider stand was locked and her two large signs which she had painted herself were down. I was getting back into my car when I spotted her walking through a field toward her house. I greeted her and explained that I was doing a book about the roadside. She paused and replied softly with this poem:

"There are hermit souls that dwell apart with peace and self
    content
But let me live in a house by the side of the road
I'll be a friend to man."

It's a great long poem and when I was a little girl, we were forced, ya know, in school to memorize all that stuff. And really it enriches your life. And nearly every day one of these old poems that we had to learn fits in.

*You told me you came to New Mexico in a covered wagon.*

I did.

*Where did you come from?*

We drove down here from South Dakota to...

*To where?*

Albuquerque. Let's see. I guess we left Dakota in about 1915. And then it took a year and a half to get here.

*A year and a half!*

Yeah.

*What were the roads like, just trails?*

Well...dirt roads.

*Were there places to stop?*

Well, in the big towns they was what they called wagon yards. You see there was very, very few automobiles. There was a few Model T's, a few Maxwells, and a few Packards. And there was a few Buicks...but they cost so much, see. It wasn't until about 1920 that Henry Ford got to making the Model T and you could buy one for about $500. And a couple of men could pick 'em up and carry 'em you know, they were so light. And uh...we could have had a Model T, but uh...my father was sickly, you see. He had asthma, bronchial trouble, heart trouble. So the doctor told him just to load up his wagon and just start going southwest... mostly south. And then he said that when you get to a place where you can breathe...you'll be going slow enough that it won't be too hard on your heart and then you will know that you can live there. While if you go in a car, you'll make about thirty miles a day...fifty miles a day was a BIG day.

*Well, how old were you then?*

Well, let me see (chuckling), let me see. I was about ten. Oh, I remember everythin' nearly. Did you want to get some cider?

*Yeah.*

I'd better get the keys. I'll tell ya...I learned a long time ago... make my sale and then do the talkin'.

*When I talked to you before, they were going to make you take down your signs.*

Oh yeah, they did. They made me take down my two best signs that was way up the road. They cut my business in half. And then the years kinda piled up on me too, so I'm not open...not so much anymore...only on Sunday and Saturday. My get-up-and-go got up and got.

My mother she was quite a lady. And she always would tell us some little something or other, or quote a funny little poem or sing a little song or something. My father and mother, they had nine children. But in that cold country they only raised three of us hardy little brats.

We had what they called Chautauqua that used to come to our little town and they come with a tent and give these long, high spiels, you know. It was really something to go to that Chautauqua tent you know. So I begged my mother till I got the money to go to Chautauqua. (she laughs) It was the most boring thing I...talkin' away and away and...I don't know what they were talkin' about! I really don't have any idea (she chuckles) what they were talkin' about. Oh dear, I was only about in the third grade, you know.

(She points to a hill of red ants.) Now, if one of them things bites you, you'll know it. And I'll tell you, the best thing to put on is a cake of ice. Oh! one of them bit me through the top of my shoe. Well, I just screamed and it just hurts like nothing you

# 5 Gassing up along the way

44

# 6

## Be sure to see...
the longest, the highest, the oldest, the newest,
the first, the only, the most unusual,
the biggest and the best

## Whoa, you missed it!

n the Nevada desert near Lovelock an Indian who calls
himself Roaring Mountain Thunder has been building a
monument to the "early peoples of America." People
nsidered it a ridiculous idea and insisted that he could
survive the harsh elements without water close at hand.
has brought in water from nearby Thunder Mountain,
d showed me his garden which supplies him with fresh
getables. As much as anything, his monument, built of
ne, concrete, and scrap, stands by the roadside to show
t almost anything is possible.

51

# 7
# Ruins
# of a
# recent
# past

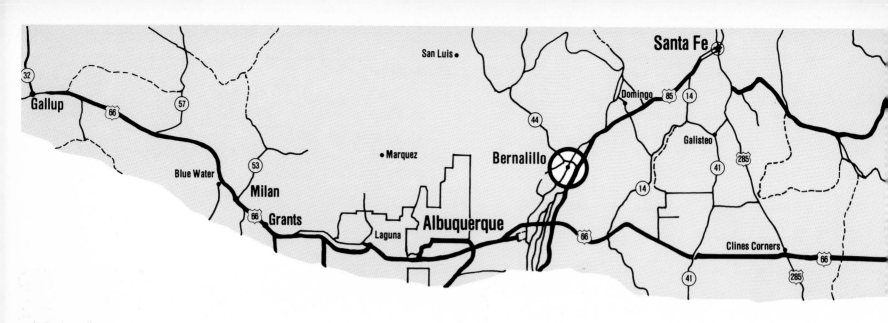

# The neon west

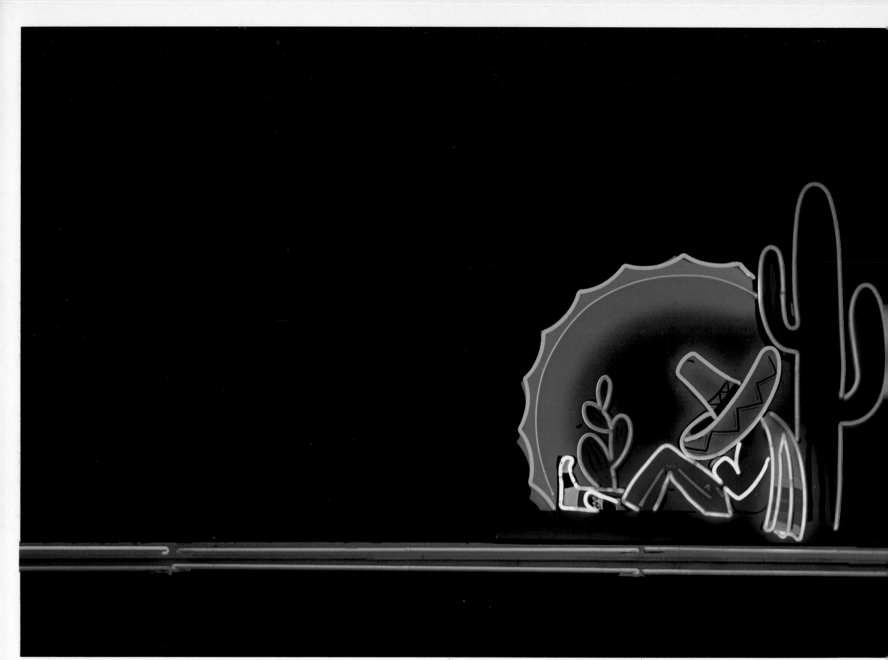

Out west, the smallest crossroad towns are usually well ornamented with a twisted array of neon tubes. Even the most mundane places on the bleakest roads often will be unexpectedly exciting in the neon night. Perhaps, it alludes to a wilder, more glamorous life somewhere else, but there it is. Illusions of far and different places are evoked by a variety of symbols and names. There are neon waves and palm trees, and places called: Iceberg Cafe, Boston Cafe, Tropics Bar, Arctic Circle... However, in a region which relies so heavily on tourism, it is more common to find neon cowboys, Indians, sombreros, cacti...and names such as: Yucca Cafe, Cactus Bar, Cowboy Cafe, Rosa's Cantina, Apache Motel, Desert Rest, and Bobcat Bite.

At dusk, the eastern sky counterpoints a brilliant western sunset with soft pinks and blues on the horizon. In a similar way, the neon signs quietly glow with pastel colors, going almost unnoticed in the passing of daylight. As the sky darkens, they gradually become garish solicitations to stop and eat, drink, and spend the night. For those traveling in the vast, western night, there is a comfort in the neon reassurance that someone is there to satisfy your every need. Neon seems appropriate and surprisingly very western in this region where land, sky, and light are so dramatic and overwhelming.

# Epilogue

One year in the early Seventies I was driving back east for Christmas. I took a convenient back road which veered northeast from Tucumcari. As I drove through the small town of Logan, New Mexico, I passed an incredible looking motel-cafe-curio shop called Casa Blanca. Though I was in a hurry, I turned around and stopped for a bowl of homemade soup. I stayed and talked for two hours with the owners, June and Joe Hettinger. The cafe was warm and filled with wonderful memorabilia that they had collected over the years. A picture of John F. Kennedy hung, centered over the old wooden counter. Outside under the south portico, there was a huge, finely painted mural which depicted the history of the state from Sandia Man into the atomic age. Casa Blanca may well be the most loved and cared for place that I've ever chanced upon in the west.

Late in the summer of 1975 I returned. I was surprised to find that the entire roadside complex was for sale and that the Hettingers were retiring. Not many tourists travel Route 54 through Logan anymore and making this sort of living so far from the interstate is difficult. The cafe was closed then but they allowed me to photograph it once more.

Like each scene in the mural outside, or like the billboard image of cowboys riding the western range, their roadside oasis is now also painted into this region's history.

From this valley they say you are leaving
We shall miss your bright eyes and sweet smile
For you take with you all of the sunshine
That has brightened our pathway awhile.

Then come set by my side if you love me
Do not hasten to bid me adieu
Just remember the Red River Valley
And the cowboy that's loved you so true.

For a long time my darling I've waited
For the sweet words you never would say
Now at last all my fond hopes have vanished
For they say that you're going away.

Then come set by my side if you love me
Do not hasten to bid me adieu
Just remember the Red River Valley
And the cowboy that's loved you so true.